1st STEPS

For New Believers

To Mary,
May God bless you
as you bless others!
Love in Christ,
Charlie

Book 1 in the series:

Becoming More Like Jesus

More books in this series coming soon:

Amazing Love — October

The Laws of God

The Basics of the Christian Faith

1st STEPS
For New Believers

Book 1 in the Series:
Becoming More Like Jesus

- A Bible-Based Study for New Christians

- No previous Bible Knowledge needed

- Teaching you the Basics of the Christian Faith in everyday language

- Non-Denominational

M. C. "Charlie" Mathis

becoming-more-like-jesus@outlook.com

Acknowledgements

I would like to thank all those who have helped in making this book become a reality. My gratitude and love go out to my Savior Jesus Christ for giving me the opportunity to follow my dream. Without Your saving grace and loving encouragement this series would never have even gotten started.

Thank you to my family, my friends, my co-workers, and my Family in Christ for putting up with me and my constant talk about "the book".

The Discipleship Training class at New Season Church deserves a special thank you as they allowed me to use them as a sounding board and to get their input in the topics that needed to be addressed.

Thank you to Jennifer Massa who proof read all my drafts and gave me positive feedback and advice for corrective action. Without your input things would look a lot differently.

My thanks also go out to Gwen Gordon and Jana Floyd for their artistic advice and for taking the pictures in my head and designing the cover with them. Visual arts are so not my thing! Without you the book may never have gotten a cover.

One last thank you goes out to CreateSpace for making it possible for this book to be published.

M. "Charlie" Mathis

Contents

Introduction: My reasons for writing these lessons

May I tell you how this study came to be? I went to church all my life, even before I received Christ as my Savior. I knew some things about the Bible and Christianity even though I was not intimately familiar with either. I became a born-again Christian in May of 1979 and was baptized that summer. A few years later I started teaching children through Sunday School, Vacation Bible School, and Children's Church. In 1997 I took a class on spiritual gifts that let me recognize that my spiritual gift was teaching. At the same time God brought me through a tough time in my personal life and I learned to depend on Him like never before.

The church I attended allowed me to teach adults, but only with their pre-approved curriculum. I had issues with that! How can thousands of people in hundreds of churches all have the same need at the same time? Most people weren't even on the same level of spiritual maturity. Therein lay a big problem as there was nothing available to teach them to grow up from new-born babies in Christ to more mature Christians. I was looking for something that everyone could understand, but that got more challenging as the students progressed in their studies.

In 2009 I changed churches under God's guidance. Here I had the freedom to teach as God led me. But I was still unable to find books or lessons that fulfilled the void I was looking to fill – the growing up of newborn Christians who have no previous Bible knowledge. This is where the vision of a one year Bible study originated. The lessons are grouped together in units (books) that have the same theme. They start out by making sure that you understand what salvation is all about and how to start your journey as a Christian. They continue through you learning the basics of the Christian Faith and using your knowledge to become a productive Christian instead of just a "bench-warmer". Each unit or book can be studied independently, but may produce better results if the lessons are studied consecutively as they build on the material that was taught in previous lessons. It would really help if you could learn in a group setting, instead of just on your own. That way everyone can share their own life-experiences, problems or victories, and you can help each other and learn from one another.

This Discipleship Training is by no means all inclusive, but ongoing: It gives you a solid foundation on which you can build to never stop growing as a Christian. Thank you for your interest in the "Becoming More Like Jesus" Discipleship Training Series. May God bless you as you grow to be more and more like Him in your character, your words, your deeds, and most of all your love for God and people!

Love in Christ,
Your sister Charlie

1st STEPS

For New Believers

Book 1 in the series:

Becoming More Like Jesus

1 - Why we should study our Bible and how

I am so excited that you are here to learn about God. He loves you so much and He is ecstatic that you have accepted Him as your Savior. Not only has He saved us, but He gave all of us a "Love-Letter" and an "Instruction Manual" to help us live an awesome Christian life. We call that book the Holy Bible. Give me some reasons why you might think we should study our Bible. If you do not feel Bible study is important please tell us why you feel that way.

The Bible is a big book which contains an enormous amount of information. So, does Bible-study sound overwhelming to you? Are you discouraged before you have even begun? Why or why not?

We will take it one step at a time and let God speak to us as we study. But in order to find a specific scripture in the Bible you have to know the "address" of it. The address is always written in the same style: first the book is listed (you can find out in the index which page it starts on), than the chapter and last the verse is listed. For example, we are about to look up a scripture in the 2nd letter to Timothy in chapter2, verse 15, where the Bible itself gives us a good reason for reading and studying it. The address would be 2.Timothy 2:15. Here is what it says (NKJV): **15** *Study to show yourself approved unto God, a workman that does not need to be ashamed, rightly dividing the word of truth.*

In one translation it says to "study" in another it says to "work hard". But what does that mean for us?

This verse also tells us that we are only responsible to God. It does not matter what people say about your study habits, only what God says! Does it tell you why you should study?

Next we will look at Genesis 3:1. Genesis is the very first book in your Bible. Here is what it says:

1 *The serpent was the shrewdest of all the wild animals the* LORD *God had made. One day he asked the woman, "Did God really say you must not eat the fruit from any of the trees in the garden?"*

How is this question phrased that is put to Eve?

Clearly, the first step our spiritual enemy takes to lead us astray is to make us doubt what the Scripture says and thereby what God says. That is why it is so important to learn more about the Bible for ourselves! It is important to know that God wants us to understand what He has to say. I always take the Bible literally unless it tells me that it is a parable (a story that explains a principle) or something else like it.

Things that will help you to study your Bible:

- Using a Bible that you can understand when you read it. There are several good translations out there. If you are not sure which one works for you, go to a Christian bookstore or to www.biblegateway.com and check it out. There you can search the scriptures by looking up Bible passages or key words. For an easy to understand translation I would recommend the New Living Translation or NLT for short, which we will be using throughout this study. I will use the New King James Version or NKJV of the Bible, where wording seems to be easier to understand in a different translation. But whatever translation of the Bible you choose to use is totally up to you, just make sure you understand what it says.

- An open mind to what God has to tell you. Pray that He will open your understanding of the Scriptures and give you the willingness to learn.
- 4 different colored pencils to mark Bible passages (i.e. red, yellow, green and blue) or special markers that won't bleed through the pages. We will practice using those today, so you can get an idea of how that part of reading your Bible works.
- One other study tool that might be helpful to you is a concordance. It is a directory that lists every word in the Bible and where it appears in the scriptures, the "address". Sometimes a partial concordance is included with your Bible. If you get them separately, make sure it is for the same translation as your Bible is (if your Bible is NIV, make sure the concordance is for the NIV Bible).

But really, the only 2 things you have to have to study the Bible are: a Bible that you can read and understand and a willingness to listen to and learn from God's Word. So, let's get started.

The Importance of the Bible

The Bible is an amazing book. It is God's holy, inspired Word and is commonly called The Holy Bible, The Living Word, or The Word of God. It is a library of 66 books, written by 40 different people over a period of 2000 years, under the divine inspiration of the Holy Spirit.
In 2.Timothy 3:16-17 (NKJV) we see why the Bible is so important. Here we read:
16 *All Scripture is given by <u>inspiration</u> of God, and is <u>profitable</u> for doctrine, for reproof, for correction, for*

instruction in righteousness, **17***that the man* (or woman) *of God may be complete, thoroughly* <u>*equipped for every good work*</u>*."*

Let's look at another translation to get a better understanding of this, and to give you an example of how the meaning is the same in all the translations, even if the wording might be different. In the NLT the same Scripture reads like this:

16 *All Scripture is* <u>*inspired by God*</u> *and is* <u>*useful*</u> *to teach us what is true and to make us realize what is wrong in our lives. It corrects us when we are wrong and teaches us to do what is right.***17** *God uses it to* <u>*prepare and equip his people to do every good work*</u>.

- It is _____ by God, not man- made.
- It is useful _____
- It is relevant and practical for:
    1.   Doctrine/Truth – teaching what we believe and why we believe it
    2.   Reproof/Wrong – show what is right and what is wrong
    3.   Correction – to fix it from wrong to right
    4.   Instruction/Teaching – training in WWJD (What would Jesus Do?)

So the reasons we should study are to mature ourselves in our faith and to learn to become all God wants us to be. Once you have finished these "First Steps" lessons, I want to encourage you to continue your studies of "Becoming more like Jesus". The lessons build on one another and will help you learn the basics of the Christian

Faith. I would also like to encourage you to find a Bible-believing Church where you can grow into a loving Christian by becoming active for Christ. Do you have any questions or comments so far?

The Central Theme of the Bible

Jesus is the central figure of the Bible. His birth as the Jewish Messiah and Savior of the world was prophesied in the Old Testament (everything that happened before Christ came to earth) which was written in Hebrew. The New Testament was written in Greek and Aramaic. In it (everything since Christ came to earth) Jesus fulfilled 100% of all the Old Testament predictions of His birth, life, death, and resurrection. Let me show you an example of this.

In Isaiah 7:14 we can read the Prophesy of the birth of Jesus.

14 All right then, the Lord himself will give you the sign. Look! The virgin will conceive a child! She will give birth to a son and will call him Immanuel (which means 'God is with us').

Then in Matthew 1 we read about the fulfillment of this Prophesy.

18 This is how Jesus the Messiah was born. His mother, Mary, was engaged to be married to Joseph. But before the marriage took place, while she was still a virgin, she became pregnant through the power of the Holy Spirit.19 Joseph, her fiancé, was a good man and did not *want to disgrace her publicly, so he decided to break the engagement quietly.***20** *As he considered this, an angel of the Lord appeared to him in a dream. "Joseph, son of David," the angel said, "do not be afraid to take Mary as your wife. For the child within her was conceived by the Holy Spirit.***21** *And she will have a son, and you are to name him Jesus, for he will save his people from their sins."***22** *All of this occurred to fulfill the Lord's message through his prophet:*

23 *"Look! The virgin will conceive a child! She will give birth to a son, and they will call him Immanuel, which means 'God is with us.'"*

Look at the Prophesy and compare it to the actual event. How many points of exactness can you find?

There are literally hundreds of Prophesies concerning Jesus that have already come true, and some we are still waiting for, like His return as our King.

We will have a more in depth lesson just on what the Bible is all about in the book: "The Basics of the Christian Faith". I hope you will join us for those lessons as well.

Throughout the Bible we see examples of how God interacts with His people. It also shows us how God takes care of His children. Jesus shows us how we can get back to God. He is the One who provided the way back to God through what we call salvation.

How to study

There are several different ways to study your Bible. As you mature in your faith, you can study people, places, themes, and so forth. But right now we will concentrate on just listening to God, as we read His Word. While you read a passage in your Bible ask yourself the following questions:

1. Can this scripture be used to lead someone to Christ? (yellow – like the streets of gold in heaven)
2. Does it give a warning or tell me to avoid doing something? (red – stop and pay attention)
3. Does it give a promise to me? (blue – Royalty – God's Character and His promises to us as His children)
4. Does it tell me to do something as a Christian? (green – go, get off your "blessed assurance" and do something)

This is the reason colored pencils will be so helpful to you. As you read your Bible, let God talk to you. And as you understand something, mark it in your Bible to help you remember it. This will also help you find it again when you need it.

For practice, we will read the 1st chapter of the book of John from verse 1 through verse 18 together and each one of us will mark it as we come across a verse that falls into one of the above mentioned categories.

1 In the beginning the Word already existed. The Word was with God, and the Word was God.2 He existed in the beginning with God.3 God created everything through him, and nothing was created except through him.4 The Word gave life to everything that was created, and his life brought light to everyone.5 The light shines in the darkness, and the darkness can never extinguish it. 6 God sent a man, John the Baptist, 7 to tell about the light so that everyone might believe because of his testimony.8 John himself was not the light; he was simply a witness to tell about the light.9 The one who is the true light, who gives light to everyone, was coming into the world.10 He came into the very world he created, but the world didn't recognize him.11 He came to his own people, and even they rejected him.12 But to all who believed him and accepted him, he gave the right to become children of God.13 They are reborn—not with a physical birth resulting from human passion or plan, but a birth that comes from God.14 So the Word became human and made his home among us. He was full of unfailing love and faithfulness. And we have seen his glory, the glory of the Father's one and only Son.15 John testified about him when he shouted to the crowds, "This is the one I was talking about when I said, 'Someone is coming after me who is far greater than I am, for he existed long before me.'"16 From his abundance we have all received one gracious blessing after another. 17 For the law was given through Moses, but God's unfailing love and faithfulness came through Jesus Christ.18 No one has ever seen God. But the one and only Son is himself God and is near to the Father's heart. He has revealed God to us.

If you ever come across a Scripture that you have questions about, please discuss it in your study group. Others may have the same question that you do. You may also want to talk with your group leader or your pastor.

To see how this passage might look, I included how I marked mine. Then we can discuss why we marked each passage. Remember, this is not a right or wrong kind of assignment. It is just how you hear God talking to you through the pages in your Bible.

Usually it is easier to find something when it is highlighted, especially if you are consistent in which colors you use for specific topics. So, let's discuss how and why we marked these passages the way we did.

Which passages did you mark yellow to help someone understand about salvation?

This is what I marked: *"to all who believed Him and accepted Him, He gave the right to become children of God. They are reborn"*

My reason for marking it: It tells me who can become a child of God – another way of saying: who can be saved.

Did you mark anything in red? Did this passage contain any warnings?

This is what I marked: nothing. To me there was no warning included here.

Did you see anything that showed a characteristic that we might want to imitate as Christians? Something we should go out and actually do? If so, what did you mark in green?

This is what I marked: *"a witness to tell about the light"*
My reason for marking it: John did something that showed other people who Jesus was. Maybe I should do the same thing.

What about blue? Did you see anything that showed you God's unchanging character or a special promise He gave you?

This is what I marked: - *"The Word was with God, and the Word was God."* - *". God created everything through Him."* – *"the Word became human."* – *"God's unfailing love and faithfulness came through Jesus Christ."*
My reason for marking this: Jesus is the Word. He is God in the flesh. And through Him we can experience God's unfailing love and faithfulness. Wow! To me that is so awesome!

I am so thankful that you are here. You are probably thinking: what now? What should I do next? Let me assure you that God wants you to know Him, all the way. So, please continue reading and marking your Bible. Why don't you finish reading the book of John! He was an actual follower of Jesus and he gave us an account of what he witnessed during his time with Jesus. Another book in the Bible you may want to give a try is the book of Proverbs in the Old Testament. Here you get great advice for living in one-liners instead of story form. If you are studying this on your own, and you do not have anyone that can answer your questions, please email me at becoming-more-like-jesus@outlook.com. I will do my best to answer your questions and to help you understand the Bible so that you can grow as a Christian.

Bible Memorization

At the start of this lesson we saw that Adam and Eve were made to doubt the truth of the Word of God. One of the most important defenses against that is memorizing Scripture. Memory verses put the Word of God in your heart and no one can take that away from you. Bible study gives you the context of the Scripture. Without knowing the context of your memory verse, you may fall into the same trap of being misled that Adam and Eve did. When you learn a memory verse, make sure you understand what it says, but also what it does not say. Learn the address of your Scripture as well. That way, when someone asks you to prove to them that it is truly in the Bible, you can show them where it is without any problems.

You may argue that you can't remember these verses; or that you are too old, or too young, or too whatever. But the truth of the matter is that it is a choice we make. If something is important to us we will learn all about it. The question then becomes of how important is the Word of

God to us? How much do we love Jesus? Are we thankful enough to learn all about Him?

Remember that Jesus gave 100% of Himself as He saved us from an eternity in hell by dying an agonizing death on the cross for you and me. Can we not spend 1% of our day, which would be right at 15 minutes each day, in return to learn all we can about this wonderful Savior of ours? You have to choose to set the time aside to meet with God. Will you commit to that today? Why or why not?

So how do we memorize these verses? By repetition! Every day read the verse out loud, write it down, read it again and try to say it by heart. You will find that it is easier than you thought it would be. Once you know a verse without having to look at it, add another one to learn to it. Repeat the first one by heart and follow the same pattern of learning this next verse that you did with the first one.

Memory Verse:

11 I have hidden your word in my heart, that I might not sin against you.
Psalms 119:11 (NLT)

11 Your word I have hidden in my heart, that I might not sin against You.
Psalms 119:11 (NKJV)

2 - Having a Conversation with God (Prayer)

If you wanted to get to know a specific person, how would you go about doing that?

In order for us to get to know God we need to talk with Him as well. The best way we can learn how to do that is by following Jesus' example whenever possible. So, let's start with prayer. What exactly is prayer?

Prayer is having a conversation with God. Just like we talk to our parents or our best friend, we can go to God and talk to Him in prayer at any time and about anything. Some of our conversations may be ok to have in public, but the ones that really show our relationship with the other person are usually done in private. Do you agree or disagree, and why?

In Matthew 6:5-13, Jesus gives us an example on how to pray, or how we can talk with God. This particular Scripture is also referred to as the "Lord's Prayer". Let's look in our Bibles and read it together and see how Jesus taught prayer to His followers, the people that we know as His disciples.

5 When you pray, don't be like the hypocrites who love to pray publicly on street corners and in the synagogues where everyone can see them. I tell you the truth, that is all the reward they will ever get.6 But when you pray, go away by yourself, shut the door behind you, and pray to your Father in private. Then your Father, who sees everything, will reward you.7 "When you pray, don't babble on and on as people of other religions do. They think their prayers are answered merely by repeating their words again and again.8 Don't be like them, for your Father knows exactly what you need even before you ask him!9 Pray like this:

Our Father in heaven, may your name be kept holy.
10 May your Kingdom come soon.
May your will be done on earth, as it is in heaven.
11 Give us today the food we need,
12 and forgive us our sins, as we have forgiven those who sin against us.
13 And don't let us yield to temptation, but rescue us from the evil one.

There are several things mentioned in the first 4 verses that we should NOT do. What are they?

FYI: A hypocrite is someone who says he is something that he is not. He is a pretender.

    a.   Why should we not repeat things over and over?

    b.   What does He mean by that 'they have their reward'?

    c.   Don't be like whom? And why?

    d.   Is there anything listed that we should do?

All these things Jesus told us before He ever talked about how we should actually pray. How does He start out this prayer? Since prayer is a conversation with God, He addresses His prayer to God. What does He call God? _____. That means you have to be _____ in order for you to call Him "Father". Is He your heavenly Father? Are you sure that you are saved? If you have any doubts at all, now would be the perfect time to ask God to forgive you of all your sins and to accept Jesus as your personal Savior. You can do that right now or right after class. Talk to your group leader or pastor or email me at becoming-more-like-jesus@outlook.com with any questions. Please don't put it off. We are talking about your eternity here.

Now we will look at each part of the prayer by itself. *May your name be kept holy*: What does "holy" mean?

If you said holy means sacred, you are absolutely correct. It also means having a character that evokes reverence. Jesus is telling us here to have respect not only for God, but for speaking His name as well. What does that mean for you?

May your kingdom come soon: God's kingdom is coming! The question really is: are we looking forward to Christ's return or not? Are we prepared for it? Are we a mission field (lost without Christ) or are we missionaries (saved by Christ and passing on that awesome good news of salvation)?

Hopefully you can count yourself among the missionaries, those that have accepted Christ as their Savior. If you have not accepted this free gift of salvation yet, it is not too late. Please don't leave here without knowing – not hoping or guessing – but really knowing that you are saved.

May your will be done on earth as it is in heaven. What does that mean? It says that God's will is being done in heaven, but not necessarily on earth. Jesus wants us to ask in prayer for God's will to be done here on earth. And what does it have to do with us? Can we influence that in any way?

I believe that yes, we can have an influence concerning God's will here on earth. I can choose to follow Jesus in my speech, my actions and my attitudes. I can choose to be obedient to His Word, the Bible. I can choose to share my experience of salvation with others. And so can you! As each one of us chooses to be the best Christian we can be we can make a difference, one person at a time.

Give us today our daily bread or the food we need. I like the way it reads in the "Message" (a transliteration of the Bible): *"keep us alive with 3 square meals"*. There is a Scripture in the Old Testament that fits right in with this. Let's read what it says in Proverbs 30:8-9.

8 First, help me never to tell a lie. Second, give me neither poverty nor riches! Give me just enough to satisfy my needs.9 For if I grow rich, I may deny you and say, "Who is the LORD?" And if I am too poor, I may steal and thus insult God's holy name.

What are we asking God for? What does God want us to do here?

We are really asking God to provide us with our daily necessities. On the other hand we are also learning to trust Him to provide that food each and every day. The key words here are "today, and daily". You see, tomorrow is not today. Next week is not today either. We shouldn't ask for our needs, like food, for the future, but only for one day at a time. And that takes trust in God. Jesus wants us to learn to trust God with the basics in life. Is there any discussion on that?

And forgive us our sins, as we have forgiven those who sin against us. Can you put this statement into your own words?

I love the fact that we can come to God and ask Him for forgiveness. The Scripture in 1.John 1:8-9 confirms this. It says:
8 If we claim we have no sin, we are only fooling ourselves and not living in the truth.9 But if we confess our sins to him, he is faithful and just to forgive us our sins and to cleanse us from all wickedness.

Both of these Scriptures, the one in Matthew and the one in 1. John, are conditional promises. That means we have to do something in order for God to do something. Please name the condition and the resulting promise for each of these two Scriptures and discuss the implications in your group.

My input for your discussion is that it is darn hard to forgive. As a matter of fact, I am struggling with that every single day of my life. But in order to become more like Jesus I need to learn to forgive the way God forgives, unconditionally! What are your thoughts?

Don't lead us into temptation nor let us yield to it, but deliver us from the evil one.
Let's read James 1:13-14 in conjunction with that:
13 And remember, when you are being tempted, do not say, "God is tempting me." God is never tempted to do wrong, and he never tempts anyone else.14 Temptation comes from our own desires, which entice us and drag us away.
Why would the Bible say in one place for Him to not lead us into temptation and in another we are told He never tempts anyone?

You are right. We are asking God's help in staying out of temptation. We are also asking for His help if we are already being tempted and have to deal with it. And that is just what He wants to do for us, help us! He is just waiting for us to ask Him for His help.

Always remember that prayer is a conversation between you and God. It does not have to be stilted, or awkward, or uncomfortable. Instead it should be open and honest. You can tell God anything! You can talk to Him any way you want to. He can handle it, I promise you. There have been plenty of times when I argued with Him. He still loves me! I just want to encourage you that as you talk to Him, let Him talk to you as well through reading your Bible and meditate on His Word.

We have looked at the model for prayer that Jesus gave to his followers. You do not have to copy that prayer word for word even though you can. Here is a simple acrostic (A-C-T-S) that might help you with your own prayers, to make them more personal between you and your heavenly Father:

A   – Adoration (of who God is)

C   – Confession (daily leaving your sin with God and asking His forgiveness)

T   – Thanksgiving (for the things He has already done and is about to do)

S   – Supplication (asking for any need you may have or help that you may need or lifting up someone else in their need)

Come on! Let's take the time to practice this A-C-T-S of prayer right here in this group. Don't make it complicated. He is your heavenly Father, your Daddy, and He just wants to be part of your life. The more you let Him into your life, the more He can help you in any situation. Prayer and Bible Study are perfect ways for you to communicate with one another. My prayer for you is that you will enjoy His company as much as He enjoys yours!

Memory Verse:

9 Pray like this:
Our Father in heaven, may your name be kept holy.10 May your Kingdom come soon. May your will be done on earth, as it is in heaven.11 Give us today the food we need, 12 and forgive us our sins, as we have forgiven those who sin against us.13 And don't let us yield to temptation, but rescue us from the evil one.
Matthew 6:9-13 (NLT)

9 In this manner therefore pray:
Our Father in heaven, Hallowed be your name.10 Your Kingdom come. Your will be done on earth as it is in heaven.11 Give us this day our daily bread, 12 and forgive us our debts, as we forgive our debtors.13 And do not lead us into temptation, but deliver us from the evil one. For Yours is the kingdom and the power and the glory forever. Amen.
Matthew 6:9-13 (NKJV)

(Some of the original manuscripts omit the last sentence, some include it.)

3 - Do I need God? If so, for what?

      You are probably thinking that this is a strange question to ask in a Bible study or in a church that proclaims to be a "Christian" church. We are not here to assume anything, or discuss church doctrine and beliefs or what people say, but only what the Bible says. If you have never received Christ as your Savior, and you have no clue what that means, you may very well have asked yourself or others: "Do I need God? And if so, what for?" I am so glad you asked. May I introduce you to the designer and maker of the universe, the King of Kings, my heavenly Father, and my very Best Friend? His name is Jesus.

      You and I, my friend, were made by Him. In Psalms 139:13-14 it says this:

13 You made all the delicate, inner parts of my body and knit me together in my mother's womb.14 Thank you for making me so wonderfully complex! Your workmanship is marvelous – how well I know it.

What do these verses tell us?

God designed us and He knew us before we were even born. It also means that since He made us, none of us are here by accident; neither are we an afterthought on God's part, or a mistake. In His eyes we are precious, wonderful, the best part of His creation, because God doesn't make junk!!!

Now look at Colossians 1:16 where it says:

16 *For through Christ (Jesus) God created everything. ...Everything was created through Him and for Him.*

How is this verse different from the previous one?

Here we are not only told that God made us; but we have a purpose as well. We were made for Him. What do you think that means?

It means that we were designed to have a relationship with God. Until we fulfill the purpose of our being by having this personal relationship with God, we will always be seeking the meaning of life for us and everyone else. Only God can fill that void. In the story of the creation of the world, in Genesis 1-3, we read how God made every living thing. For people, whom He made in His own image, He prepared a special garden in which to live. He arranged it so that Adam and Eve could meet with Him there every day, to share their daily experiences with Him, and to just be close to Him. He still wants that for all of us today, to find that special place where we can just meet with Him, and be with Him and enjoy each others' company. But something happened that changed all that. SIN! Can you explain what sin is? Maybe you can give some examples?

Sin is doing something against the will of God and the purpose He has for our lives. But what has sin got to do with us not being able to be with Jesus the way He intended?

In breaking one of the laws of God, sin sets up a barrier between God and people. In Romans 6:23 God says that *The wages of sin is death.*
In other words someone has to die for messing up. Here we see that there is a severe consequence for sin – death. So then, logically speaking, if I am the one that sinned, I have to die. Correct? Yes and no! Yes, because I am the one that messed up and deserve to die. And no, because God did not create us just to turn right around and kill us again. He still wants to be with us, have a close relationship with us, and be our Savior and Friend.
In Romans 3:23, God tells us
For everyone has sinned; we all fall short of God's glorious standard.

You do realize that this verse includes all of us, you, me, your pastor and mine, Billy Graham, Mother Teresa, and every other person in the whole world, right?

You might argue that you are not really THAT bad. Well, both of us know that either we have sinned or we have not. In God's eyes there is no such thing as a little sin or a big sin. Just like there is no such thing as being just a little bit pregnant. Either you are or you are not. So, have you ever sinned?

Well, your next question might be: Now what? How can I make things right again between God and myself? Do you think that God might break, or at least stretch, His own law enough to help one of us out?

This is not something He will do, nor can He, as it would violate His own laws. In other words we messed things up but we have no way to fix it! But God has provided a way that we do not have to die. Someone else had to die in our place though, a substitute. That someone else is His only son, Jesus. Jesus never sinned so He did not have to die for His own sin. But because He loves us like crazy, He chose to die for my sin and yours. Can you believe that? Can you believe this kind of love actually exists? How awesome is that! Let's read about it together in John 3:16-17.

16 *"For God loved the world so much that he gave his one and only Son, so that everyone who believes in him will not perish but have eternal life.* **17** *God sent his Son into the* *world not to judge the world, but to save the world through him.*

And the second part of Romans 6:23 tells us that *The free gift of God is eternal life through Jesus Christ our Lord.*

You probably think that this is one of those things that sound too good to be true. What's the catch? What do you think?

There is no catch! You do not have to do anything to be accepted by God. Remember, He made you and me because He loves us, and wants to have a relationship with us. The Bible in Romans 5:8 reminds us of that:

8 But God showed His great love for us by sending Christ to die for us while we were still sinners.

What does that mean?

It simply means that God not only loves us after we accept Him as our Savior, but He loved us from the very beginning. Like with any other gift, we must personally receive this free gift of salvation to make it our own. This is what the Scripture in Romans 10:9-13 talks about.

9 If you confess with your mouth that Jesus is Lord and believe in your heart that God raised him from the dead, you will be saved.10 For it is by believing in your heart that you are made right with God, and it is by confessing with your mouth that you are saved.11 As the Scriptures tell us,

"Anyone who trusts in him will never be disgraced." **12** *Jew and Gentile are the same in this respect. They have the same Lord, who gives generously to all who call on him.* **13** *For "Everyone who calls on the name of the LORD will be saved."*

What is your part in this, what do you have to do? Say it in your own words:

Ephesians 2:8-9 reminds us that
8 *God saved you by his grace when you believed. And you can't take credit for this; it is a gift from God.* **9** *Salvation is not a reward for the good things we have done, so none of us can boast about it.*

According to this Scripture, what do we have to do to earn salvation? _____

Nothing! There is absolutely nothing you can do to earn salvation. **Jesus paid the price! It is a free gift for us!** Do you know how I know? Because "grace" means getting something that I do not deserve! And with all the sins in my life I surely deserved to die – we are talking about our spirit here, not our bodies – but now I won't. Because Jesus died for me! And He did the same for you! I have one last question for you: What happens when we mess up again? What happens when we sin again after we have accepted Christ as our Savior? What will happen to our salvation? If you are not sure about the answer, read

John 3:16 -17 again! There is a key word in it that should help you find your answers. What is that key word? And what is the conclusion we can draw from that?

Did you find that key word? It is: eternal. Salvation means you receive eternal life. We will study this subject in more detail in the book: The Basics of the Christian Faith. For now, we can find assurance of our salvation in Hebrew 10:10 where it says

10 *For God's will was for us to be made holy by the sacrifice of the body of Jesus Christ, once for all time.*

WOW! Not only does God choose to love and save us, but He also keeps us safe for all eternity. If you have never accepted Jesus as your Savior, but you want to, I would like to invite you to pray with me right now: "Lord Jesus, I know that I have sinned. I also know that according to your law I deserve to die. But I am sorry for my sins and I repent of them. I believe that Jesus died for me and rose again. I really mean this with all my heart and I am asking you to save me. Thank you for saving me. Help me to live the life of a true Christian. " If you meant this prayer with all your heart, than you are saved, or born again, like it is also called in the Bible. Please let someone (this class, your pastor, your family ...) know what Jesus has done for you, so that all of us can rejoice with you.

<u>Conclusion</u>:

After what we have learned in this lesson, what is your answer to the questions of whether we need God and if so, for what.

I believe you are right when you say that yes, we need God. Not for religion, but for relationship! He designed us to be in a close relationship with Him. Mankind messes that up with sin. But God loves us so much, that He steps right in to rescue us from the consequences of our sin. Jesus bled and died for us, so that we might have a chance at a restored relationship with God. On top of that, God leaves the choice of accepting this free gift of salvation up to us. He basically said:"I love you enough to die for you. Do you love Me enough to accept My gift of salvation to you?" When it is put it like that, than yes, we need God because He is the only one who can provide the solution to our problem with sin. I am just so glad that I serve a God who loves me THAT much! How about you?

Memory Verse

16 *"For God loved the world so much that he gave his one and only Son, so that everyone who believes in him will not perish but have eternal life.*
John 3:16 (NLT)

16 *"For God so loved the world that He gave His only begotten Son, that whoever believes in Him should not perish but have everlasting life.*
John 3:16 (NKJV)

4 - Worshipping God

The dictionary informs us that the word worship means to love, admire and respect someone unquestioningly and to show that devotion thorough our actions. According to this definition, is there someone or something in your life that you worship?

Your answer may have been an emphatic NO. Or you may have been honest enough to realize that there are things in all of our lives that we worship. For some of us it may be our job, or money and the power it brings with it, or what about celebrities? The Bible talks about worshipping God. And when you read the passages that mention worshipping Him, there are 3 things that keep being mentioned with it:

- to bow down
- prayer
- sacrifice

We will look at each of these individually. But for now we just want to share the meaning of these things for us as Christians and our how they relate to our worship of God. Discuss your ideas!

There are countless ways to express our worship for God. We have just named some of them. But there is another word we will look at besides expression of our worship and that is the essence of our worship.

- The expression of our worship is based on us: our personality; our likes and dislikes; our...
- The essence of our worship is ALWAYS based on God: who He is; His likes and dislikes; ...

So let's start at the beginning. Do you love, admire and respect God unquestioningly and without reservations? Why or why not?

As for me, I definitely love God for all that He has done and is still doing for me. I admire Him for the variety of His creation. And I respect Him for knowing what is best for all of us. But I have lots of questions and doubts. Does that mean that I can't worship Him? Give a reason for your answer.

It just means that I have questions and doubts. It means that I do not know or even begin to understand all there is to know about God. It means that I am still getting to know Him, just like you are. Then how do we show God through our actions how much we love Him and the respect that we have for Him? We do that through our _____. Worship is the outward expression of what is in our hearts.

Let's look at some scriptures and see what they reveal to us about worship.

Matthew 2:11 – *"They* (the wise men from the east) *entered the house and saw the child* (Baby Jesus) *with his mother, Mary, and they* <u>bowed down</u> *and worshiped him."*
What is the significance of bowing down? Do we still do so today and if so, when and why?

I agree that we still bow down to dignitaries for instance. We do so out of the respect that we have for the office they hold. Another instance where someone might bow down is when a POW returns home. When his feet hit home ground he may very well fall to his knees and even kiss the ground. His actions are not so much out of respect, but out of love, the love for his country and the freedom that country represents. Both of these examples are highly significant. They hold lots of meaning for the one performing the act of bowing down. Now it might be easier to see why the wise men bowed down to Jesus. Discuss this and also ways that we can worship God by "bowing down" as an expression of our worship. What would be the significance of that.

Luke 2:37 – *"She* (an old widow) *never left the Temple but stayed there day and night, worshiping God with fasting and prayer."*

We have already learned the meaning of prayer in our previous lesson. But what does fasting mean?

Fasting is the act of giving something up in the physical realm in order to gain something else in the spiritual realm. For instance, we may fast by not eating food for a day. This is not done for the purpose of losing weight, which is also something physical, but for the purpose of showing God that we trust Him to take care of us. In our example, as you give up food, what is your spiritual gain? Nothing yet! You need to replace it with a spiritual practice like prayer. Name some other physical things we might give up in order to show God our seriousness concerning the prayer that is attached to the fast.

Fasting is usually combined with a very specific prayer. We are asking God's help with a special matter through our prayer and the fasting shows God that we are serious about this prayer and that we trust Him to deal with it His way and in His time; not the way we want it dealt with. Fasting and prayer show God how much we care about Him. It is a powerful and personal expression of what is in our hearts. Is there any discussion on this or does anyone have any questions?

John 4:23 – "true *worshippers will worship the Father in spirit and in truth.*"

What does that mean? Think about what the opposite of that would be for example?

The opposite of a true worshipper to my understanding would be a hypocrite. Someone that expresses his "worship" without having the love of God in his heart! The expression of our worship is supposed to come out of the overflow or the essence of our worship which are our salvation and love for God. Without having Christ as our Savior, there is no essence – no love for God – that would prompt us to show Him our love in the expression of worship. Have I confused you yet? Remember from our lesson on salvation that a hypocrite is a pretender. In this case he would pretend to worship God while in truth he doesn't even know God. So his worship is based on a lie. Are you a pretender? If so, would you like to change that? Would you like to have the love of God in your heart and your sins forgiven?

If you do, then ask God to forgive you of your sins right now. Tell Him that you accept Jesus as your Lord and Savior. Ask Him to help you to grow as a Christian. If you truly mean what you have just said, then God has saved you. Please let all of us rejoice with you, by letting us know of this change in you.

Did you know that there is rejoicing in the presence of the angels of God over your decision? In Luke 15:10 we read that

There is joy in the presence of God's angels when even one sinner repents.

How awesome is that!!! I have been trying to tell you that God is thrilled with your acceptance of Him, with your decision to accept Him as your Lord and Savior. To me this previous Scripture sounds like: "Party-time" in heaven! And all because of you and your acceptance of God's free gift of salvation!!! Thinking about that gets me all excited for you!

Romans 12:1 – *"And so, dear brothers and sisters, I plead with you to give your bodies to God because of all he has done for you. Let them be a <u>living and holy sacrifice</u>— the kind he will find acceptable. This is truly the way to worship him.*

I hate to sound ignorant, but aren't sacrifices usually dead? What would be considered a living sacrifice?

I heard an old proverb one time that kind of went like this: If someone saves my life then I owe that person my life. I think that is a really good example of a living sacrifice. Jesus saved our lives. Now we owe Him those lives. If we truly believe that and let Him work in us to be the best Christians we can be, then that becomes an awesome expression of our worship. Can you give some examples of a life of "living sacrifice"? How would it be different than living without God?

After looking at all these scriptures, what can we conclude about worship?

- It shows our _____ for God
- It is not _____, but active. Worship is an ACTION verb.
- We _____ God with our service for Him.
- In order to worship Him, we need to stay in constant _____ with Him.
- The expression of our worship (outward) should be a reflection of the _____ of our worship (what is in my heart).

- A living sacrifice means giving up _____ and accepting God's will for my life, and living accordingly.
- Acknowledging that everything we are and everything we have is from God.

You may see other things that are important to worship, so please list them here:

Some people have the idea that in order to worship God they have to do certain things or act a certain way. But I am here to tell you that your worship has <u>nothing</u> to do with any of the following:

- A type of music
- A style of service
- A denomination
- A certain translation of the Bible
- How we dress or look
- Pleasing people instead of God

Some of these things are traditions with which we have grown up. That doesn't make them right or wrong. It just means that we have gotten into a habit of doing something a certain way. Yet sometimes we fall into the trap of believing that we are the only ones who are doing things the right way. <u>Worship is all about God, not us</u>. It is our adoration of Him. It's like having a "can't help it" that just has to come out because our hearts are so full of love for Him. Our worship is focused on Him, not us or others. It is a matter of the heart in every sense of the word. It is personal, because it is a reflection of who I am, not who you think I should be. The same holds true for you!

Your worship of God is your personal expression of your love for God.

Memory Verse

1 And so, dear brothers and sisters, I plead with you to give your bodies to God because of all he has done for you. Let them be a living and holy sacrifice—the kind he will find acceptable. This is truly the way to worship him. 2 Don't copy the behavior and customs of this world, but let God transform you into a new person by changing the way you think. Then you will learn to know God's will for you, which is good and pleasing and perfect.
Romans 12:1-2 (NLT)

1 I beseech you therefore, brethren, by the mercies of God, that you present your bodies a living sacrifice, holy, acceptable unto God, which is your reasonable service. 2 And do not be conformed to this world, but be transformed by the renewing of your mind, that you may prove what is that good, and acceptable, and perfect, will of God.
Romans 12:1-2 (NKJV)

5 – Now what? What are my next steps?

I am so proud of you that you have completed this whole book. It is not easy being a new Christian. Hopefully I was able to help you in some small way to take your first steps on your journey to becoming more like Jesus.

This is not really a lesson, but some useful information in looking for a church home and continuing your walk with God. I hope that by this time you have finished reading the book of John and have found lots of things to mark that God has pointed out to you. I also pray that you have started "hiding God's Word in your heart" by memorizing some Scriptures. Why don't you take the time right now to go over your memory verses and discuss how they have influenced your thinking?

I think it is extraordinary that the God of the universe chooses to communicate with each one of us through the pages of the Bible.

Next, I would encourage you to read the book of Acts which comes right after the book of John. Here we see the start of the Church as Christians spread the Gospel or the Good News that Jesus is the Savior of the world.

If you have not found a church home yet, don't be afraid or intimidated to try out some different churches. Ask your friends, family and co-workers where they go to church. Go with them a couple of times when they go to church and see what it is like. Here are some things that I looked for when God moved me to my new church home:

- The preaching and teaching has to be biblical. You have to be able to see the truth of the Bible reflected in what is being said and understand what is being taught. I will include a list of Christian beliefs that are a must for any Church that proclaims to be a Christian church.

- The invitation to salvation is given at every opportunity. This should be explained so that anyone seeking God can understand what salvation means and how to receive Christ as their Savior. There should also be some kind of follow-up to help new Christians grow in their faith.

- The Love of God should be openly displayed by the people attending this church, not just by the people in leadership. John 13:35 tells us how others can know whether we are true Christians or hypocrites:

^{35} Your __love__ for one another __will prove__ to the world that you are my disciples.

I know that it is not an easy process to look for, find, and decide to join a church. I had to do it myself in 2009. But I want to promise you that God will help you if you ask Him to. By giving you these guidelines I just want to ensure that your church agrees with what the Bible teaches, not what people say! Anytime you bring different people together you are going to get differences of opinions. Don't get carried away by those opinions, but stand firm on the truths of your Bible!

Here is the list of essential Christian Beliefs that should be the same in any Christian Church, regardless of people's opinions:

God

We believe that there is but one God, omnipotent, omniscient, omnipresent, who is the Creator and Sustainer of all things, visible and invisible, revealed in three Persons: Father, Son and Holy Spirit.

The Father

We believe in God the Father, the Ancient of Days, who is not aloof from human history but who, through various covenants, has initiated a relationship with mankind, and to whom we have now been reconciled through the sacrifice of Jesus Christ upon the Cross. Because of Jesus Christ, we too can now call God "Father."

The Lord Jesus Christ

We believe in the Lord Jesus Christ, His deity, His virgin birth, that He died, was buried and on the third day rose back to life. He ascended to heaven and is now seated at the right hand of the Father. We believe that He is the eternal Son of God, for whom and by whom all things were created.

The Holy Spirit

We believe that the Holy Spirit (as the third Person of the triune God) proceeded from the Father and the Son, and is of one substance, majesty and glory with the Father and the Son.

The Holy Scriptures

We believe in the divine inspiration of the Holy Scriptures, contained in the Old and New Testaments of the Bible, as the sole revelation of the mind and will of God. And we accept them as the divine Word of God.

The Devil

We believe that the Devil, through temptation and deception, initiated the downfall of man. And he now seeks to destroy the faith of every believer in the Lord Jesus Christ and to hinder the further spread of the Gospel of salvation through Jesus Christ.

Justification by Faith

We believe that it is impossible to attain salvation through self-effort: But through simply believing in the atoning death and resurrection of the Lord Jesus Christ and in acting out that faith through receiving Jesus Christ as Lord and Savior, we receive the remission of all our sins, reconciliation with God and the gift of eternal life. We hold that the believer has an eternal salvation secured in Christ.

Sanctification

We believe it is the glorious privilege of every believer in Christ to be made pure in heart and wholly sanctified by the operation of the Holy Spirit through the blood of Christ and the Word of God. A believer cannot be justified by works, but evidences that justification through works empowered by the Holy Spirit.

The Church

We believe in the Church of the Lord Jesus Christ, made up of all who have believed, through the ages and everywhere, on the Lord Jesus and received the salvation of the Cross, and that this Church will come to the full expression of unity that can only be found in the Gospel of Jesus Christ, according to the prayer of Jesus Christ in John 17. *

Two words I would like to explain just in case you are unfamiliar with them. The first one is "justification" or being "justified". The best explanation I have ever heard for this is that it stands for "just as if I'd never sinned". It means that when God looks at you He sees you as if you had never sinned; just like Jesus. The other word I would like to explain is "sanctification". It means to be made holy through the Holy Spirit in us. I hope that these clarifications will help you to understand the significance of these essential **Statements of Faith** mentioned above.

You might wonder what to make of all the different denominations within the Christian Church. Regardless of denomination, the preceding Statements of Faith are believed by all of us. Denominations are not of God, but of men. Denominations focus on differences of opinions concerning non-essential beliefs within the Scriptures. God focuses on unity in the faith. If you read the prayer that Jesus prayed in John 17 you will see the truth of this.

And as always, you can contact me with any questions or concerns about this. Just send me an email at becoming-more-like-jesus@outlook.com.

Memory Verse
35 *Your love for one another will prove to the world that you are my disciples.*
John 13:35 (NLT)

35 *"By this all will know that you are My disciples, if you have love for one another".*
John 13:35 (NKJV)

May God help you with these decisions and may He bless you just as you have blessed me! My hope and prayer for your future are that you will never stop growing in your Love for God and people; and that your hunger for God and His Word will never grow cold. If you are interested in learning more about God, I would love to walk with you some more on your way to Christian maturity. "Amazing Love" is book 2 in the series of "Becoming More Like Jesus". I hope to experience this with you as well.

> Love in Christ,
> Your sister Charlie

*The preceding Statements of Faith were adapted from the Ames International School of Ministry's Website and are used by permission.

Recommended Reading:

- The Practice of the Presence of God by Brother Lawrence – This book contains the journey of Brother Lawrence to make prayer not a separate part of his life, but an attitude of being in constant communication with God.
- What the Bible is all about by Henrietta Mears – This book gives insight into each book of the Bible and what it is all about, its highlights, stories, and important points to remember.
- In His Steps by Charles Sheldon – It shows what happened when people chose to ask "What would Jesus do?" before they make any decisions.

Resources:
I added these online resources for your convenience. They all have large amounts of information that can help you in your growth as a Christian.

http://www.wordsearchbible.com
http://www.apologeticspress.org
http://www.blueletterbible.com
http://www.biblegateway.com
http://www.youversion.com

About myself

     I was born in 1961 in Mainz, Germany and lived there until 1981 at which time I moved to the USA. I am number six out of seven children and the middle daughter. Mom is of the Lutheran faith and dad is a Seven-Day Adventist. As children we were sent to mom's church, not taken. Because of that and other circumstances we had lots of confusion and stress within the whole family. I felt like I never measured up to the accomplishments of my siblings or the expectations of my parents or teachers. My self esteem was practically non-existent. On top of that, at the age of ten I already looked like I was sixteen, fitting in with neither age group. I was searching for a person or place to be accepted for who I am. Dad was always reading his Bible, so I gave that a try as well. God showed me a verse in 1.Samuel 16:7 that drew me to Him. It says:

People judge by outward appearance, but the Lord *looks at the heart.*

For the first time in my life I felt that I had a chance of being accepted! By reading more in my Bible, God showed me that He did not judge me by my looks, nor by my accomplishments (or the lack thereof), but by what is in my heart. Shortly after that I heard the message of salvation for the first time at a Missionary Baptist Church, even though I had gone to church all my life. In May of 1979 I accepted Jesus as my Savior. What a change! What a joy!

Jeff and I got married in January of 1980, while he was still stationed in Mainz, and I was still in high school. In 1981 our beautiful daughter Rebecca was born and several months later Jeff's tour in Germany was over. We moved to Powder Springs, Georgia, to live with his parents while we were looking for our own place. Let me tell you that that was quite a culture shock for me. Once again I felt totally out of place and very much alone. Our wonderful son Daniel was born in 1985.

Through many different circumstances in our lives we had an on again, off again kind of thing going about attending church. In 1997 God intervened in our lives and separated us so that I could grow in my faith in Him, instead of putting my faith in Jeff. Once again my self esteem was shattered and I had to start all over again. It was a difficult 7 ½ years to say the least. But looking back I can see that I finally became ok with who I was. I learned to accept myself for who God made me. What a breakthrough!

You might ask for my credentials for writing these lessons, and I confess that all I have to show for in that regard are my Love for God and for His Word and the strong desire to teach new Christians in order for them to have a solid foundation in their faith. I am still learning new things daily myself. But what I have learned I feel the need to pass on. I have taught children and adults in all the churches were I have served. To this day I teach these same lessons that you are reading here in my home church. Quite a large amount of the materials in these books stem from the questions that come up during the discussions in our group! I hope and pray that they will answer your questions as well.

I may never have the opportunity to meet you in person while we are still on this earth. But I am sure looking forward to meeting you in Heaven. Until we meet, I would like to leave you with the words of an old hymn:

Oh, don't go away without Jesus.
Oh, don't go away without Him.
You know He is willing to save you,
And cleanse from your heart every sin.
So yield to His offer of mercy,
And take of the grace He imparts.
But don't go away without Jesus,
In your heart.

(Author unknown)

Love in Christ,
Your sister Charlie